National Curriculum
Key Stage 2 Age 10–11

Practice Papers

Key Stage 2
National Tests

ENGLISH

How the Key Stage 2 National Tests will affect your child

- All pupils in Year 6 (age 10–11) will take National Tests in English, Mathematics and Science. These important tests are held in May each year and are designed to be an objective assessment of the work your child will have done during Key Stage 2 of the National Curriculum.

- Pupils will also have their school work assessed by their teachers. These teacher assessments will be set alongside your child's results in the National Tests to give a clear picture of his/her overall achievement.

- In July, the results of your child's tests together with the teacher assessments will be reported to you.

- Results from these tests will be used in the compilation of school 'league tables'.

- It is not the purpose of the tests to aid secondary schools in deciding which children to give places to, but the results may be used to help place your child in the appropriate teaching group.

How this book will help your child

- This book offers plenty of practice in the type of question your child will face in the Key Stage 2 National Test for English, including a spelling test.

- The answers and a mark scheme have been provided to allow you to check how your child has done.

- The 'Note to parent' boxes in the Answers section give you advice on how to improve your child's answers and avoid common mistakes.

- A unique Marking grid allows you to record your child's results and estimate the level of the National Curriculum at which your child is working.

Contents

What you need to know about the National Tests

What is the purpose of National Tests?

The tests at the end of Key Stage 2, taken by pupils in Year 6, have several functions:

- they provide the government with a snapshot picture of attainment throughout the country, enabling it to make judgements about whether standards are improving nationally;
- they give information to OFSTED about schools' achievements, so that they can judge which schools are improving and which are deemed to be failing their pupils;
- they give you information about your child's progress compared to national standards.

How do the tests work?

In May of Year 6, your child will take tests in the core subjects of English, Mathematics and Science. In English, there are tests for Reading, Writing and Spelling. The Reading and Writing Tests take about an hour to complete (including preparation time) and the Spelling Test is completed in about 10 minutes. The tests are not marked in school by a teacher, but posted off to an external marker, who is often a teacher in another school or a retired teacher. External markers have been trained in marking the tests so that the pupils' test papers throughout the country are marked to the same standard.

Once the tests have been marked, the mark is translated into a 'level'. The level that each mark corresponds to is decided according to results gained in pre-tests and the tests themselves. It varies slightly from year to year. The test papers, marks and levels are returned to your child's school in July, then the levels are reported to you and to the secondary school that your child will attend.

What do the tests assess?

The tests are designed to assess your child's knowledge, skills and understanding in the context of the programme of study for English at Key Stage 2 set out in the National Curriculum. This can be found on the National Curriculum website, www.nc.uk.net. The programme of study is divided into three sections, called Attainment Targets:

- En1 – Speaking and Listening
- En2 – Reading
- En3 – Writing.

The written tests assess En2 and En3. Your child's teacher assesses En1.

What are the levels and what do they mean?

There is a set of benchmark standards that measure a pupil's progress through the first three Key Stages of the National Curriculum. Attainment is measured in steps called 'levels', from 1 to 7. The National Curriculum document sets out the knowledge, skills and understanding that pupils should demonstrate at each level. The government target is for pupils to achieve level 2 at the end of Key Stage 1, level 4 at the end of Key Stage 2 and level 5 or 6 at the end of Key Stage 3. The chart below shows these government targets.

How your child should progress

At the end of Key Stage 2, most pupils take the tests targeted at levels 3 to 5. High attaining pupils will also take these tests but will be able to achieve a Gifted and Talented level, which will show that they have achieved a very high score in the national tests. To achieve a Gifted and Talented level your child will need to be very advanced in his/her studies compared to most pupils of this age.

How does this book help my child?

This book gives your child practice in answering the type of question that he/she will face in the actual tests. By practising questions in this way, your child will feel under less pressure and be more relaxed. Being relaxed helps pupils to perform at their best in tests, so we have targeted the questions at levels 3–5, allowing your child to become familiar with most of the types of question that are asked in the tests. We have also included some additional questions in the reading tests (marked with an asterisk) to give your child practice in tackling the more difficult types of questions that would achieve a Gifted and Talented level in Reading. The marking framework for Writing also provides guidance on achieving a Gifted and Talented level.

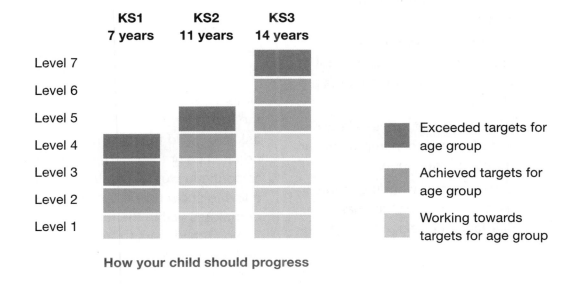

How your child should progress

Preparing and practising for the English Test

The questions in this book will help your child to prepare for the Key Stage 2 English test. The National Curriculum divides English into three elements: Speaking and Listening, Reading and Writing (including spelling). The Key Stage 2 English test comprises a Reading Test, a Writing Test and a Spelling Test. The speaking and listening element is not tested, but your child's teacher assesses this as part of the statutory teacher assessment.

What are the key features of this book?

This book contains all you need to prepare your child for the tests:

- National Curriculum requirements – key information for each of the Attainment Targets En2 (Reading) and En3 (Writing).

- Questions – practice test papers targeted at levels 3–5 in Reading, Writing and Spelling.

- Answers – showing the responses that will gain credit in the tests and how the marks are allocated.

- 'Note to parent' boxes – advice as to how you can improve your child's performance.

- Level charts – what the marks mean in terms of National Curriculum levels.

How should I use this book?

Well in advance of the tests, suggest to your child that some practice might be a good idea. Make sure that he/she is in comfortable surroundings and has all the necessary equipment (pen, pencil, rubber and ruler).

The Reading Test

Detach the marked pages from the back of this book and fasten them together to make the English Booklet. Read through the instructions on pages 9–11 together. Spend some time making sure that your child understands the instructions for completing the test and then leave your child alone for the specified time (15 minutes) to read the booklet. During this time, be available to help interpret instructions, but do not look over your child's shoulder as this may prevent him/her from concentrating fully. You might want to suggest that your child reads *Camping and Survival* on pages 2–7 of the English Booklet first but emphasise that your child is not meant to memorise the readings; he/she may refer to the booklet at any time during the test.

Note the starting time in the box at the top of the test. After 45 minutes, ask your child to stop writing. If he/she has not finished, but wishes to continue working on the test, draw a line to show how much has been completed within the test time. Then let your child work to the end of the test, but check that he/she is able to cope with the questions as they become more difficult.

The Writing Tests

There are two Writing Tests and an assessment of handwriting. To set the Writing Tests, make sure your child has some writing paper. Read through the instructions on page 21 together. You should allow your child 10 minutes to plan for the first Writing Test. Note the starting time at the top of the first sheet of writing paper. Remind your child that his/her handwriting will be assessed in this test as well. After 40 minutes, ask your child to stop writing.

The second Writing Test takes 20 minutes. Your child should think briefly about what they want to write but not write down their planning. Handwriting is not assessed in this test.

The Spelling Test

The Spelling Test requires you to detach page 14 of the English Booklet and read out a story to your child. Your child will be asked to fill in the missing words on his or her version of the story on page 27. The test should take about 10 minutes.

How to mark the tests

After your child has completed the Reading Test, work through the paper along with the answers and advice at the back of the book. Record your child's marks in the top half of the boxes in the margin. Work out the total marks gained for each question, write them in the Marking grid on

page 48 and add them up to arrive at the total mark for the paper. You can then use the charts on page 47 to determine the level of your child's performance on this test.

If your child required extra time to complete the test, go through all the questions with your child, but do not include the marks for the 'extra' questions in the score.

Go on to mark the other tests and fill in the Marking grid in the same way.

If your child tends to work slowly, you can encourage him/her to use time more effectively:

- identify specific amounts of time needed to complete sections of a test, e.g. 10 minutes to plan the first Writing Test;

- if your child is struggling with a question, ask him/her to read it through aloud, then ask if your child knows what the question means – this often helps clarify whether or not he/she can respond to the question;

- encourage your child to move on to the next question if he/she gets really stuck;

- identify areas of the Reading Test where questions are easier – usually the beginning of each section, e.g. pages 12 and 16.

After your child's first test, it is a good idea to highlight or make a note of areas where your child did not do well, so that he/she can revise these. Avoid extensive criticism, as this will allow your child to appreciate any suggestions as to how he/she may improve. You could encourage your child to write brief revision notes as a memory aid.

What does the level mean?

The tests in this book give a guide as to the level that your child is likely to achieve in the actual tests. We hope that, through practice, these tests will give your child the confidence to achieve his/her best. By working through the answers with your child, you should be able to improve his/her achievement.

So that you can compare your child's achievement with national standards, the chart below shows the percentage of pupils awarded each level in 2002.

How do I help my child prepare to take the actual tests?

A few days before the test:

- check that your child knows which test papers he/she will be taking, and when these are to be sat;
- work through practice questions and discuss which answers are right and why;
- double check that your child has the necessary equipment, including a spare pen and pencil.

Finally, avoid putting your child under pressure and reassure him/her about any worries that he/she may have.

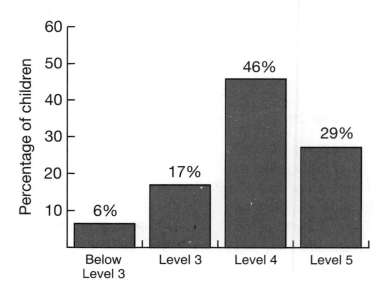

Levels in English in 2002

Reading Test
Level 3–5

INSTRUCTIONS

Carefully detach pages 1–12 of the English Booklet at the back of this book. Fasten the pages together to make your own English Booklet. The test is divided into two parts: *Camping and Survival* (an informative passage about camping) and an extract from *Island of the Blue Dolphins* (the true story of a young American Indian girl's struggle for survival).

You will have 15 minutes to read your booklet before you begin the test. You may wish to start reading *Camping and Survival* first. Don't worry if you do not finish reading the whole booklet. You may look at the booklet as often as you wish during the test.

The main written part of this test should take about 45 minutes. If you know from your teacher at school that you are working at level 3 or level 4 in reading, you should tackle all questions *except* those marked with an asterisk (*). If your teacher has told you that you are working at level 5 in reading, then you should tackle *all* the questions in this test.

Read all the questions in the test carefully. In some questions you need to choose the best word or group of words to fit the passage and put a ring around your choice, for example:

The title of the story is:

Blue Island

Blue Island Dolphin

Blue Dolphin Island

Island of the Blue Dolphins

Some questions require only a word or phrase, for example:

Write down which day comes after Monday.

...tuesday...

Some questions ask for slightly longer answers. To answer these questions you will be given two or three lines, for example:

What do you enjoy doing at the weekends?

...Playing Computer games...

Some questions ask you to fill in charts, for example:

What do you like doing…	Monday	Tuesday
At school?	Science	Math
At home?	tv	tv

Some questions require a long answer. These questions often ask you to give reasons for your answer or to use the text in the English Booklet to help you to explain why you have a particular opinion. These questions will have a box for you to show your answer, for example:

Do you think that *Camping and Survival* in the English Booklet is interesting?

 Yes [✓]   No [ ]

Explain your opinion as fully as you can below.

You might like to include details about:

- whether you thought the information on camping was interesting;

- whether there was enough detail about what to eat;

- whether you are interested in camping.

....

....

....

....

....

....

Reading Test
Level 3–5

START	
FINISH	

  3h

Camping and Survival

These questions are about *Choosing a site*, *Living in a tent* and *Keeping order* (pages 2, 3 and 4).

1 When choosing a site for a tent you should try to find:

a hill   a beach   (level ground)   a river

1 Q1

2 The author says that choosing a site for a tent that is close to a suitable water supply is important for:

swimming   (cooking)   fishing   sailing

1 Q2

3 It is particularly important to be organised and tidy:

when it is warm   when it is cold   (when it is wet)   when it is sunny

1 Q3

4 It is easy to become sloppy when living in a tent when:

people have little time   people have little space

people are tired   (people are lazy)

1 Q4

5   Safety is very important when you are camping.
Give two dangers the author warns us about.

2
Q5

1   *It Invaded to gecatte*   Likely to be Invaded by came

2   *Above patu river*   Above a river

6   Look at *Keeping order* (page 4). The following things
should be done when you first make camp.
Put them in the correct order.

2
Q6

Lay out your sleeping bag and mat   4   ✗

Take off your hiking boots   3   ✗

Sort out the cooking arrangements   2   ✓

Pitch the tent   1   ✓

7   Here are two pieces of advice from *Keeping order*.
Explain why each one is important.

2
Q7

Don't take out any more than you need from your backpack.	*help keep the tent tidy it*
Don't crowd into a tent or move around clumsily.	*avoid the tent sheet*

9
Max. 10
Qs 1–7
subtotal

13

8 'Take off hiking boots before you go into the tent.'
What **two** reasons does the author give for
doing this?

1 ...They can damage The ground
Sheet

2 ...becuse It Going to to diy
tent

These questions are from *What to eat* and *Backwoods cooking* (pages 5 and 6).

9 'Tins and bottles are unsuitable.'
Why does the author state this?

becuse it going to be vey
heavey when you carry them

10 Some sorts of wood should never be used for making
skewers to cook food.
Why does the author say this?

becuse The cauld be poisoniu

11 Non-fiction books are often written for a particular readership.
Who do you think is likely to read *Camping and Survival*?

Describe clearly the type of person and the situation for which the information would be useful.

Information useful for	Dog frictan reader
Type of person	3rd person
Situation	test wood

***12** Some of the information in *Camping and Survival* is presented in paragraphs, bullet points and illustrations.
Why do you think the author has chosen to present information in this way and is it effective?

The Saey first Section give a
Good checklst of Stafety

3
Q*13

Max. 23
Qs 1–*13
subtotal

*13 You have been asked to rewrite the *What to eat* section (page 5) using bullet points.
Organise the information into the **five** most important points.

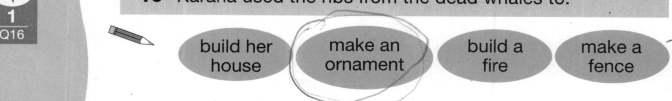

- .... totally Mensus Should be worked out
- .... Carry food that leight waright
- ....
- ....
- ....

Island of the Blue Dolphins

1
Q14

14 Karana needed to build her home in a place that was:

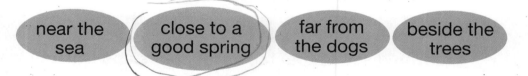

near the sea   (close to a good spring)   far from the dogs   beside the trees

1
Q15

15 The sea elephant bulls often weigh as much as:

a large house   a big rock   (thirty men)   a bus

1
Q16

16 Karana used the ribs from the dead whales to:

build her house   (make an ornament)   build a fire   make a fence

17 Look at page 9.
Choose and copy **two** words that tell us the kind of noise the sea elephants made.

2
Q17

.......Screaming.....and..bagging.........

....

18 The author describes the sea elephants as 'just hundreds of specks against the waves' (page 9). Explain what this phrase tells you about the sea elephants.

2
Q18

......because 1..There...was..lot..of.

.........anmiad....a...against..The..waves

19 'I felt that the day was an omen of good fortune' (page 9).
Which of these explanations gives the best idea of what this sentence means? Choose and tick **one**.

1
Q19

The weather was good that day. ☐

Karana was feeling happy. ✓

Karana thought things would go well. ✓

The day was good for singing. ☐

Max. 8
Qs
14–19
subtotal

2
Q20

20 Karana had to use things that were on the island to help her to survive.
Draw lines to match the things Karana used to the way they helped her to survive. One has been done for you.

Karana used ...

whale ribs

wood and rock

a tight basket of fine reeds

a flat rock

to ...

cook shellfish and perch

build a fence

build her house

cook seeds

1
Q21

21 Karana built the fence first.
Why did she decide to do this?

So the ___ing aniamal dont come

3
Q22

22 Look at the illustration of the house and fence.
Write down **three** details from the story that helped the artist to draw this picture.

Whale ribs Pointed

a rock for the back Of the base

four poles of walls

23 The author has chosen to write this story in a particular way.
Choose the **best** word to complete the following sentence.

This story is rather like a ……… *diary* ……….

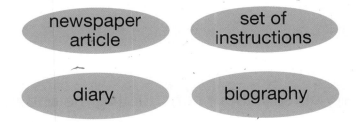

newspaper article

set of instructions

diary

biography

24 How do you think the author wants us to feel about Karana?
a Circle **one** of the following.

Karana is:

independent   nervous   savage   greedy

b Find **two** clues in the story to support your opinion.

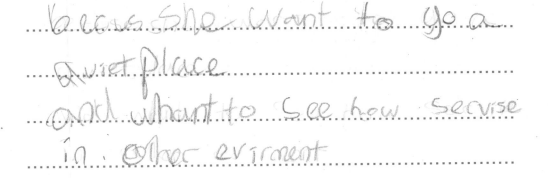

becaus she want to go a quiet place and whant to see how servise in other evirment

3
Q*25

*25 Which of the two possible sites for Karana's house had a better water supply?
Explain why this was.

Keweenoe retaised that the water supply was better att the other place than at the highlands. This was becuse the stream flowed more steady

3
Q*26

*26 Karana was very careful about constructing the entrance to her house.
Identify **three** things that she did. Explain how each of them helped to make Karana's home more secure.

1 ....

2 ....

3 ....

Max. 24
Qs
14–*26
subtotal

Camping and Survival and **Island of the Blue Dolphins**

3
Q27

27 Do you think that the author of *Camping and Survival* would have approved of the steps that Karana took to survive on Blue Dolphin Island?
Explain the reasons for your answer.

Yes beauuse to Make More Intresting

....

Max. 3
Q27
subtotal

20

Writing Tests

INSTRUCTIONS

Make sure that your parent has read the notes on page 7 before you begin the Writing Tests. Then read the instructions below.

On pages 23 and 25 there are two Writing Tests. You must complete both of them during the hour allowed for these Tests.

Read through both starting points, 'Missing!' and 'Lost!', with your parent.

Completing the story 'Missing!'

You should complete 'Missing!' first. Your parent will give you some paper. Write your name and the title 'Missing!' at the top of the first sheet.

You will have 10 minutes to plan your writing. Using the planning frame to help you, make notes about how to:

- start your story in an interesting way;
- get into the story quickly;
- make sure the order of events is clear;
- include only a small number of characters;
- plan a convincing ending.

Remember that planning should help you to get your ideas for writing in order. You will not be marked on your plan. Try to write your ideas quickly: you do not have to use full sentences.

You should then take a further 30 minutes to complete this first Test.

Your handwriting in the 'Missing!' story will be assessed after you have finished the Test.

Completing the second Writing Test 'Lost!'

Your parent will give you another clean piece of paper. Write your name and the title 'Lost!'

Look at the ideas on 'Lost!' that have been included in this book to help you.

You should **not** plan this writing by making notes.

You should spend a little time thinking about the details that you wish to include in your notice.

You will have 20 minutes to complete this second Writing Test.

Writing Tests
Level 3–5

START

FINISH

Complete both Writing Test 1 and Writing Test 2.

Writing Test 1

Missing!

There was silence, except for the sound of the wind whistling around the tent. Chris called frantically, but Alex was nowhere to be seen.

Use your imagination to write what has happened, from Chris's point of view.

Remember to take care with your **handwriting** in this first Test.

PLANNING SHEET

Use this space to jot down your ideas before you begin. The questions may help you sort out your ideas.

Where were Chris and Alex and why?

What had happened at first?

How did Chris react to what happened?

What had happened to Alex?

How did it all turn out in the end?

Writing Test 2

Lost!

Something – or someone – is lost.

Write a notice to put in your local paper to ask for help.

Remember: you will need to think about the details below before you begin and to set out the notice in a way that will attract people's attention. Use the ideas below to help you.

- who or what's lost;

- when and where last seen;

- description;

- how to get in touch;

- reward.

Your handwriting is **not** assessed in this second Test.

Spelling Test
Level 3–5

INSTRUCTIONS

This Spelling Test will take about 10 minutes.

Your parent will read the story on page 14 of the English Booklet out loud twice. You will follow along with your version of the story on page 27, which has some words missing.

As your parent reads the story out loud for the first time, follow along with your version, but do not write anything.

Your parent will read the story for the second time. When you come to a gap, wait for your parent to read you the word. Write the missing word on the line. If you are not sure how to spell the word, just try to write the letters you think are correct.

SPELLING TEST

You have probably often _heard_ ✓ people say that food always tastes better out of doors.

wheather it's because of the open air or because you're _especially_ hungry after walking, it certainly seems to be true that campers usually have a _healty_ appetite. ✗

If you are camping for any _length_ ✓ of time, you will need to cook, or at least heat, food and water while you are away from home. Here is some basic advice about _preparing_ ✗ a meal.

Be sure that you take _Particular_ ✓ care when starting a fire, _Sellctrag_ ✓ your spot so that there is no risk to surrounding _country Side_. Never _leave_ your fire unattended in any circumstances. A moment of _carelessnes_ can give rise to a major fire, which may _destroy_ trees, plants, wildlife and even homes.

You may _Choose_ to cook simply, heating up _Pocket ket_ meals or frying eggs and bacon, or you may wish to do some real 'backwoods cooking'. _Although_ it sounds rather strange, food will cook slowly if it is first heated _hroughly_ ✗, then buried in the ground with hot coals or embers. Of course, the food should be in a container or _wrapped_ ✓ in foil. You don't want to eat a _Hoth mourful_ ✓ of earth!

Finally, don't _forget_ ✓ the washing up. There's no need to carry a bowl, as you can _Scoop_ ✓ out a hole in the ground and line it with a plastic bag.

Answers

HOW TO MARK THE READING TEST

Re-read the English Booklet before marking your child's answer to the Reading Test. This will help to clarify the marking scheme and will also help you to judge whether the content of an answer is correct. Different children have different ways of wording a correct answer – you need to judge whether your child 'had the right idea'.

***Choosing a site, Living in a tent** and **Keeping order** pages 2, 3 and 4*

1	level ground	*1 mark*
2	cooking	*1 mark*
3	when it is wet	*1 mark*
4	people are lazy	*1 mark*

5 *Award 1 mark for any of the following points:*

- falling branches from trees
- falling rocks
- cattle
- flooding
- high tides

Up to 2 marks

6 The correct order is:

Lay out your sleeping bag and mat	4
Take off your hiking boots	3
Sort out the cooking arrangements	2
Pitch your tent	1

Award 1 mark for two correct answers.
Award 2 marks for four correct answers.

Up to 2 marks

7

Don't take out any more than you need from your backpack.	*Helps keep the tent tidy.*	*1 mark*
Don't crowd into a tent or move around clumsily.	*Avoids the inner sheet being pushed against the flysheet, which can lead to the rain coming into the tent.*	*1 mark*

Up to 2 marks

8   *Award 1 mark for each of the following:*
  - the boots bring in mud and wet
  - the boots can damage the groundsheet

Up to 2 marks

What to eat and **Backwoods cooking** (pages 5 and 6)

9   - they are heavy to carry
  - they are not compact

Award 2 marks for answers that reflect both of the above points.
Award 1 mark where only one reason is given.

Up to 2 marks

10 It is poisonous.   *1 mark*

11

Information useful for		
Type of person	*a young or inexperienced camper*	*1 mark*
Situation	*preparing/planning to go camping and in need of detailed advice*	*1 mark*

Up to 2 marks

12 *Award 1 mark for answers that refer to the text giving instructions or being set out to help the reader.*
Award 2 marks for answers that also give an example of how effective the organisation is, e.g. The 'Safety first' section gives a good checklist of safety precautions.
Award 3 marks only for answers that identify two aspects of organisation (e.g. headings, bullet points) and discuss their effectiveness.

Up to 3 marks

13 *Award 1 mark for two of the following points.*
Award 2 marks for four of the following points.
Award 3 marks for all five points.

  - You will need to eat more when you are living in the open. A normal diet should be all right on a short camping expedition, but on a longer expedition a properly balanced diet must be worked out.
  - Drink lots of liquids and take a reasonable amount of salt to prevent dehydration.
  - Eat plenty of energy-giving carbohydrate foods.
  - Carry food that is lightweight and compact to carry.
  - Daily menus should be worked out in advance and each day's rations stored separately in plastic bags.

Up to 3 marks

***Camping and Survival** subtotal up to 23 marks*

Answers: Reading

Island of the Blue Dolphins

14	close to a good spring	*1 mark*
15	thirty men	*1 mark*
16	make a fence	*1 mark*

17 *Award 1 mark for each of the following:*
- screaming
- barking

Up to 2 marks

18 *Award 1 mark for each answer that reflects the following ideas:*
- there were many sea elephants;
- the sea elephants were so far away that they appeared very small.

Up to 2 marks

19 Karana thought things would go well.   *1 mark*

20 *Award 1 mark for one correctly matched pair.*
Award 2 marks for two or three correctly matched pairs.

whale ribs   to cook shellfish and perch
wood and rock   to build a fence
a tight basket of fine reeds   to build her house
a flat rock   to cook seeds

Up to 2 marks

21 *Award 1 mark for a response that reflects the following:*
- Karana did not feel that she would be safe sleeping in her new shelter if she did not have protection from the wild dogs.

1 mark

22 *Award 1 mark for any of the following answers:*
- whale ribs pointed outwards
- a rock for the back of the house
- four poles for the walls
- eight poles for the roof
- mat over the entrance hole
- sea in the background

Up to 3 marks

23 diary   *1 mark*

24 a independent   *1 mark*

  b *Award up to 2 marks, 1 each for a suitable answer.*
    Suitable examples of Karana's independence are:

- Karana knew how to hunt for her food.

- Karana was able to build her own shelter.

- Karana made decisions about where she wanted to live.

                                                          Up to 2 marks

*25 *One mark example answer:*

The water supply at the other location was better than what
was available at the headland.

Two mark example answer:

The spring near the other site was easy to reach. There was
also less bracken and the flow of water was steadier than
it was at the headland stream.

Three mark example answer:

Karana realised that the water supply was better at the other
place than at the headland. This was because the stream
flowed more steadily than the one at the headland and was
easier to reach.

                                                          Up to 3 marks

*26 *Award 1 mark for any of the following. Answers must include
a specific example and an explanation of the way it made the
entrance to Karana's home more secure. Award up to 3 marks.*

- The tunnel was just wide enough for Karana to crawl
  through, so there was no extra space for larger animals to get
  into her home.

- The tunnel was lined with stones to prevent it getting
  larger if the soil was compacted or washed away by rain.

- A mat covered the outside entrance in order to keep
  rain out of the tunnel.

- A flat stone that Karana could push into place closed
  the end of the tunnel. This would prevent smaller wild
  animals that could get through the tunnel from getting into
  Karana's house when she was there.

                                                          Up to 3 marks

                            ***Island of the Blue Dolphins** up to 24 marks*

Camping and Survival and **Island of the Blue Dolphins**

27 This type of question requires your child to give a personal reaction to his/her reading. Refer to the Note to parent opposite for further guidance in marking this type of question. Award one mark for each reason that is supported by reference to the text.

'Yes' responses

One mark example answer.

Yes, the author of *Camping and Survival* would have approved of Karana building her shelter near a good supply of water.

Two marks example answer.

The author of *Camping and Survival* would have approved of Karana taking care to build her home in a place that was sheltered from the wind and close to a good supply of water.

Three marks example answer.

Yes, the author of *Camping and Survival* would have approved of the care that Karana took in locating her shelter. Both the locations she considered gave her protection from the wind and had access to a good supply of water. He would also have thought that she made good arrangements for cooking and storing her food.

Up to 3 marks

'No' responses

The text seems to support 'yes' answers, but if your child can find reasons to support 'no' answers, then mark them accordingly.

Up to 3 marks

Camping and Survival and **Island of the Blue Dolphins** *up to 3 marks*

Note to parent Your child is asked to respond to questions in a lot of different ways. Make sure that he/she understands how to answer questions that involve filling in charts or large boxes. If this is a problem, talk it through until your child sees how the question works.

The questions look at the text from a range of different perspectives. If your child has difficulty with a particular type of question, try to identify the main point of the question and talk that aspect through with your child. Sometimes there is more than one aspect to a question but mainly they are as follows:
- Factual, e.g. questions 1 and 6.
- Overview of the text or story, e.g. questions 10, 13 and 23.
- Deduction (sometimes using evidence from the text to support answer), e.g. questions 9 and 22.
- Commenting on characters – why they said or did particular things, e.g. question 24.
- Identifying how words have been used in the text/how the author has used language, e.g. questions 2 and 3.
- Personal response or opinion (which is often linked to questions involving an overview of the story), e.g. question 27.

Marking questions that require a personal or extended response:
- Award 1 mark where your child has given a very basic answer with little supporting textual evidence.
- Award 2 marks where your child has given a fuller answer with more detail drawn from the text, but has not demonstrated a complete response to the question.
- Award 3 marks where your child has given a full answer and their own opinion is well supported by reference to the text.

It is not expected that your child will give exactly the same answers as those given in these answers or include the same details. However, the answers given should match the demands of the examples for an award of 1, 2 or 3 marks.

If your child has difficulty with the questions that require a longer response, discuss two or three ideas that your child might include in the answer and also identify the vocabulary he/she might find useful. Get your child to 'say' his or her answer before trying to write it.

Answers: Writing

HOW TO MARK THE WRITING TESTS

There are two marking keys, the first for the story 'Missing!' and the second for the 'Lost!' notice. You should start by marking the story.

Marking the story 'Missing!'
Start by reading your child's story. Before you mark it, read it through at least twice, so that you become familiar with it. The first marking key should be used to mark the story and is on pages 36–38. The key will ask you questions about how your child has used grammar and punctuation and organised his/her writing and how effectively he/she has told the story.

After you have read the instructions below on how to use the marking key, read the example on pages 41–44 to see how Juliet's story was marked using the key for the story.

Begin with the Band 1A questions for *How well has your child used sentences and punctuation?* Tick the 'yes' or 'no' box for each question in this Band. When you answer 'yes' to all the questions in a Band go on to the next Band. When you reach a Band where you answer 'yes' to more than half the questions but not all of them, you should give the lower marks indicated for the Band. Full marks should only be given when you answer 'yes' to all the questions in a Band. Where you answer 'yes' to less than half the questions in a particular Band you should award the full marks of the previous Band. Enter the number of marks for this element on the Marking grid on page 48.

Next, answer the questions for *How well has your child structured and organised their writing?* in the same way. These questions ask you to consider how the ideas have been organised and whether there are links made between events or ideas. Enter the number of marks you award for this element on the Marking grid on page 48.

Do the same for *How effectively has your child told the story?* Note that 3 marks are available for Bands 2C, 3C and 4C. Award the lowest mark where you answer 'yes' to more than half the questions. Award the second mark where you are answering 'yes' to all but one of the questions. Award the highest mark where you say 'yes' to all of the questions. Enter the mark you award on the Marking grid on page 48.

Marking the 'Lost!' notice
Again, read through your child's writing twice to familiarise yourself with it. The second marking key on pages 39–40 should be used to mark this test. There are only two sets of questions for you to answer this time: *How well has your child organised their writing and used grammar and punctuation?* and *How effectively has your child written the notice?*

Begin with the Band 1D questions for *How well has your child organised their writing and used grammar and punctuation?* Tick the 'yes' or 'no' box as before. You will notice that only one mark is awarded for each Band. When you do not tick all the 'yes' boxes within a Band, consider whether that Band or the Band below best describes your child's writing. When you have decided on the Band, enter the marks in the Marking grid on page 48.

Then answer the questions for *How effectively has your child written the notice?* Tick the 'yes' or 'no' box for each question. When you answer 'yes' to all the questions in a Band, go on to the next Band. When you reach a Band where you answer 'yes' to more than half the questions but not all of them, you should give the lower marks indicated for the Band. Full marks should only be given when you answer 'yes' to all the questions in a Band. Where you answer 'yes' to less than half the questions in a particular Band you should award the full marks of the previous Band. Enter the number of marks on the Marking grid on page 48.

The marks from the two Writing Tests, along with the scores from the Spelling Test and the score for Handwriting (see page 44), will contribute to your child's overall level for Writing (see page 47).

Note to parent

You may notice that your child's Band for grammar and punctuation is different from his/her Band for 'organising' or 'telling' their story. It is possible to achieve different Bands for these different categories.

The marking keys show what is needed to achieve each Band. By analysing your child's writing in such detail, you will be able to see what he/she does well and where the writing needs to develop. When your child is planning other writing, discuss how he/she could take account of features that the marking key indicates could be improved. For example, if you notice that events are disjointed and do not relate well in the story your child wrote for this test, you might discuss how the events could link together sensibly when your child plans another story.

MARKING KEY: 'Missing!'

How well has your child used sentences and punctuation?	Yes	No
BAND 1A Are many of the ideas very simple (e.g. '*there are no people*') or linked by '*and/so*' or '*then*'?	☑	☐
Are capital letters and full stops used occasionally?	☑	☐
Award 1 mark if your child's writing has some of these features.		

	Yes	No
BAND 2A Is the basic grammatical structure of sentences correct (e.g. subject and verb agree)?	☐	☐
Are simple joining words such as '*but*' or '*because*' used?	☑	☐
Are simple descriptive phrases used (e.g. '*a big door*', '*he walked slowly*')?	☐	☐
Are capital letters and full stops (or exclamation or question marks) used correctly in most sentences?	☑	☐
Award 2 marks if your child's writing has some of these features.		
Award 3 marks if your child's writing has all of these features.		

	Yes	No
BAND 3A Is there some variety in sentence structure?	☑	☐
Are complex sentences used (e.g. clauses linked by '*so that*', '*although*', '*which*')?	☑	☐
Are tenses and pronouns consistent?	☐	☐
Are descriptive phrases used (e.g. '*an eerie silence*', '*tucked behind one of the boxes*')?	☑	☐
Are capital letters, full stops, question marks and exclamation marks used correctly in most cases?	☐	☐
Are commas used correctly sometimes?	☑	☐
Is there punctuation within sentences (e.g. speech marks, apostrophes)?	☑	☐
Award 4 marks if your child's writing has some of these features.		
Award 5 marks if your child's writing has all of these features.		

	Yes	No
BAND 4A Are sentences varied in length and structure?	☐	☐
Are descriptive phrases and/or subordinate clauses used to build up detail and interest?	☐	☐
Are sentences (including complex sentences) mostly grammatically correct?	☐	☐
Are capital letters, full stops, question marks and exclamation marks used correctly in almost all cases?	☐	☐
Is punctuation within sentences (dashes, brackets, colons; including the punctuation of speech and use of commas) used correctly in almost all cases?	☐	☐
Award 6 marks if your child's writing has some of these features.		
Award 7 marks if your child's writing has all of these features.		

	Yes	No
GIFTED & TALENTED Is a wide range of structures used effectively to give the writing impact?	☐	☐
Does the use of appropriate phrasing and sentencing allow the writing to convey subtle shades of meaning?	☐	☐
Is a wide range of punctuation used as appropriate to the structure of the sentences?	☐	☐
Is all punctuation accurate?	☐	☐
Award 8 marks if your child's writing has all these features.		

Answers: Writing

How well has your child structured and organised their writing?	Yes	No
BAND 1B Does the writing rely on simple connectives to show the relationship between events (e.g. 'one day', 'and/then', 'suddenly...')?	☐	☐
Are the events sequenced in a sensible order?	☐	☐
Award 1 mark if your child's writing has some of these features.		
BAND 2B Is there some indication that ideas have been organised (e.g. some grouping of ideas or sentences; beginning or end section may be a separate paragraph)?	☑	☐
Is there simple but coherent relationship between ideas (e.g. time markers such as 'before', 'as soon as', or 'an hour later')?	☑	☐
Are simple links maintained to avoid confusion, e.g. clear use of pronouns such as 'I'/'she'/'they'?	☑	☐
Award 2 marks if your child's writing has some of these features.		
Award 3 marks if your child's writing has all of these features.		
BAND 3B Does the story have a suitable opening?	☑	☐
Does the story have a clearly defined beginning, middle and ending?	☑	☐
Are events logically organised (usually chronologically)?	☑	☐
Are time/space relationships between events signalled to make for coherence (e.g. 'during the following afternoon', 'above the silent streets')?	☑	☐
Are sentences grouped to distinguish e.g. action, description, dialogue?	☑	☐
Is there use of paragraphs to mark the beginning, main events and ending?	☑	☐
Are details of where the story is set used to develop the plot?	☑	☐
Award 4 marks if your child's writing has some of these features.		
Award 5 marks if your child's writing has all of these features.		
BAND 4B Is the writing well organised and convincingly structured?	☐	☐
Is there controlled and interesting movement through the narrative (e.g. flashback, reference to events that follow)?	☐	☐
Is there variety in the relationships between ideas, e.g. contrasts in mood or pacing?	☐	☐
Are these relationships between ideas signalled in a variety of ways (e.g. a variety of connectives, adverbial phrases)?	☐	☐
Does the relationship between the paragraphs add to the cohesiveness of the story?	☐	☐
Are paragraphs used confidently?	☐	☐
Award 6 marks if your child's writing has some of these features.		
Award 7 marks if your child's writing has all of these features.		
GIFTED & TALENTED Has the text been organised to achieve a particular effect?	☐	☐
Is the story line well developed so that complications are convincingly resolved?	☐	☐
Are the various elements of the story drawn together to make a convincing conclusion?	☐	☐
Is there variety in the length and structure of individual paragraphs which add to the overall effect of the story?	☐	☐
Award 8 marks if your child's writing has all of these features.		

Answers: Writing

	How effectively has your child told the story?	Yes	No
BAND 1C	Does the writing attempt to tell a story?	☐	☐
	Does the writing have the elements of a simple story, i.e. two or more related events; one or more characters?	☐	☐
	Is there some attempt to interest the reader?	☐	☐
	Award 1 mark if your child's writing has some of these features.		
	Award 2 marks if your child's writing has all of these features.		
BAND 2C	Does the writing attempt to tell a story related to the starting point?	☑	☐
	Is there a beginning and a sequence of events?	☑	☐
	Is there an attempt to distinguish between characters, e.g. through what they say or do?	☑	☐
	Is there some inclusion of details designed to create interest, humour or suspense?	☑	☐
	Does the story have a simple ending?	☐	☐
	Award 3 marks if your child's writing has some of these features.		
	Award 4 marks if your child's writing has most of these features.		
	Award 5 marks if your child's writing has all of these features.		
BAND 3C	Is the story reasonably well paced?	☑	☐
	Does the ending relate to the main plot?	☑	☐
	Is there significant interaction between the characters (e.g. through dialogue)?	☑	☐
	Is there some development of the characters through what they say or do?	☑	☐
	Are details included to help the reader (e.g. about the setting of the story or the characters?)	☐	☐
	Award 6 marks if your child's writing has some of these features.		
	Award 7 marks if your child's writing has most of these features.		
	Award 8 marks if your child's writing has all of these features.		
BAND 4C	Are there interesting story devices, for example:	☐	☐
	• does it start with dialogue or in the middle of a dramatic event?		
	• does it include a sub-plot or a 'twist'?		
	Is the ending convincing?	☐	☐
	Is the reader's interest engaged and kept (e.g. through suspense, lively characterisation, comments on events)?	☐	☐
	Are events, description and dialogue suitably interwoven?	☐	☐
	Is Standard English used, or colloquialism or dialect used only for effect (e.g. in dialogue)?	☐	☐
	Is it a convincing story type (e.g. mystery, traditional tale)?	☐	☐
	Award 9 marks if your child's writing has some of these features.		
	Award 10 marks if your child's writing has most of these features.		
	Award 11 marks if your child's writing has all of these features.		
GIFTED & TALENTED	Does the story engage and keep the reader's interest throughout?	☐	☐
	Is the reader drawn into the story by the use of various devices e.g. imagery, metaphor and simile?	☐	☐
	Does the story have a theme (controlling idea) as well as a convincing plot?	☐	☐
	Is there an interplay between characters and events?	☐	☐
	Do the characters develop or change as a result of the story (e.g. by facing conflict or solving problems)?	☐	☐
	Are characters given substance according to their importance to the theme or plot?	☐	☐
	Are the elements drawn together to make a satisfying conclusion?	☐	☐
	Award 12 marks if your child's writing has all of these features.		

MARKING KEY: 'Lost!'

How well has your child organised their writing and used grammar and punctuation?	Yes	No
BAND 1D		
Are many of the ideas very simple (e.g. '*it mostly sleeps*') or linked by '*and/so*' or '*then*'?	☐	☐
Is there some connection between sentences?	☐	☐
Are capital letters and full stops used occasionally?	☐	☐
Award 1 mark if your child's writing has most of these features.		
BAND 2D		
Is there an attempt to organise the information (e.g. using the headings appropriately or grouping statements)?	☑	☐
Is the basic grammatical structure of sentences correct (e.g. subject and verb agree)?	☑	☐
Are simple joining words such as '*but*' or '*or*' used?	☑	☐
Are simple statements and simple instruction forms used (e.g. '*it has a blue button*', '*don't touch its ears*')?	☑	☐
Are capital letters and full stops used correctly to mark about half the sentences?	☑	☐
Award 2 marks if this level best describes the way your child has organised their writing and used grammar and punctuation.		
BAND 3D		
Is the information mainly organised into suitable sections to fit the headings?	☐	☐
Is there some variety in sentence structure?	☐	☐
Are tenses and pronouns consistent?	☐	☐
Are capital letters, full stops, question marks and exclamation marks used correctly in most cases?	☐	☐
Is there punctuation within sentences (e.g. commas, apostrophes)?	☐	☑
Award 3 marks if this level best describes the way your child has organised their writing and used grammar and punctuation.		
BAND 4D		
Are sections of the text developed around the main themes of the topic?	☐	☐
Is similar content grouped together?	☐	☐
Are sentences varied in length and structure?	☐	☐
Are sentences (including complex sentences) mostly grammatically correct?	☐	☐
Are capital letters, full stops, question marks and exclamation marks used correctly in almost all cases?	☐	☐
Is punctuation within sentences (including commas) used correctly in almost all cases?	☐	☐
Award 4 marks if this level best describes the way your child has organised their writing and used grammar and punctuation.		
GIFTED & TALENTED		
Is a wide range of structures used effectively to give the writing impact?	☐	☐
Does the use of appropriate phrasing and sentencing allow the writing to convey subtle shades of meaning?	☐	☐
Is a wide range of punctuation used as appropriate to the structure of the sentences?	☐	☐
Is all punctuation accurate?	☐	☐
Award 5 marks if this level best describes the way your child has organised their writing and used grammar and punctuation.		

Answers: Writing

How effectively has your child written the notice?	Yes	No
BAND 1E Does the writing attempt to give information? Does it include some statements or instructions, but assume the reader knows the background? **Award 1 mark if your child's writing has most of these features.**	☐ ☐	☐ ☐
BAND 2E Does the writing attempt to give information related to the starting point? Are individual statements or instructions clearly separated from one another (e.g. starting on a new line)? Is there some inclusion of details designed to give a clear picture or create interest for the reader (e.g. *'It has long floppy ears'*)? Does the writing show some understanding of what readers need to know? **Award 2 marks if your child's writing has many of these features.** **Award 3 marks if your child's writing has all of these features.**	☑ ☐ ☑ ☑	☐ ☐ ☐ ☐
BAND 3E Is the reader addressed directly (*'Are you able to help?'*)? Does the writing convey a fairly clear picture of the circumstances as well as the item lost (e.g. specifying the exact moment of loss)? Does the notice give an appropriate amount of information (i.e. not too little or too much)? Are descriptive phrases used for detail and clarity to help the reader (e.g. *'the blue lead attached to its collar'*)? Is there an attempt to give the reader significant and helpful details (e.g. full details of how to return the item)? Is there appropriate sequencing of points under each heading? **Award 4 marks if your child's writing has many of these features.** **Award 5 marks if your child's writing has all of these features.**	☐ ☐ ☐ ☐ ☐ ☐	☐ ☐ ☐ ☐ ☐ ☐
BAND 4E Is the reader's interest engaged directly (e.g. through lively imaginative touches, a convincing picture of the situation)? Are additional details included to increase the reader's understanding and/or enjoyment of the writing? Is there a suitable balance between conciseness and detail (e.g. *'my pet is very affectionate, but timid'*)? Is the tone of the notice consistent (e.g. friendly but clear)? Does the writing conform to the conventions of a real leaflet (giving a good balance of detail in an authoritative way)? Is it set out in an appropriate way (with appropriately organised information under each of the headings)? **Award 6 marks if your child's writing has many of these features.** **Award 7 marks if your child's writing has all of these features.**	☐ ☐ ☐ ☐ ☐ ☐	☐ ☐ ☐ ☐ ☐ ☐
GIFTED & TALENTED Does the notice engage and keep the reader's interest throughout? Does the piece read like a real notice (or a pastiche of the leaflet form) in every respect? Is descriptive language used precisely to give the reader specific information? **Award 8 marks if your child's writing has all of these features.**	☐ ☐ ☐	☐ ☐ ☐

SAMPLE STORY: MISSING!

Missing!

"Alex! Stop playing around and come back. Please! You haven't had any breakfast."

Chris stood for a minute wondering what to do. She wanted to think this was just Alex messing about as usual, but she felt scared and her tummy started to rumble. Even Alex wouldn't tease her for as long as this.

Alex had gone out to fetch water, but that was half an hour ago and the stream was only just behind the tent. It was no good, she would have to use the mobile phone and Mum would never let her go camping again.

"Alex! Really come back now or I'll have to call Mum. She'll be dead unhappy if she gets bothered at work and you're just mucking about. I'm going to get the mobile now."

But before she finished there was a loud noise from the woods. It was a dog barking. Out of the woods ran a man with a backpack and a pair of binoculars, being chased by a huge alsatian.

"Here, call off your dog!" he shouted, panicking.

"It's not my dog" said Chris, 'But we've got one like this at home" and she called it over. It must of smelt her dog because it came straight to her.

She patted the alsatian and it sat beside her. She felt a bit nervous seeing a stranger out here and was glad to know he was afraid of the dog.

> At that minute the owner appeared. "Don't worry" she said with a smile, "Kye's friendly really, just didn't like the look of the back pack." The man with the binoculars didn't smile back, in fact he looked grumpy. Better change the subject.
>
> "Have you seen my friend anywhere?" asked Chris, "She went off a few minutes ago."
>
> "I thought there might be somebody else around," said the dog owner. "Kye was sniffing around," said the dog-owner. "Kye was sniffing around behind the rocks over there. Let's go and have a look. I've got my mobile if we need to call for help."
>
> Thank goodness, Chris muttered to herself, this stranger seemed helpful. They all went over to the rocks and there was Alex. She was just sitting up, holding her head.
>
> "That'll teach me to play tricks!" Alex groaned. "I only meant to tease you but I slipped and fell. I must have blacked out."
>
> Chris was really relieved. She went to get some water and they all had a cup of tea.

SAMPLE MARKING OF THE FIRST WRITING TEST ('MISSING!')

How well has your child used sentences and punctuation?

Juliet's story uses a variety of sentence structures, including complex sentences (e.g. *'Chris stood for a minute wondering what to do'*). Tenses and pronouns are consistent, and there is no confusion in references to 'she'. There are some descriptive phrases (e.g. *'only just behind the tent'*). Capital letters, full stops and question marks are used correctly. Commas, speech marks and apostrophes are used, though not correctly in all cases. For this reason, 4 rather than 5 marks have been awarded to this writing.

4 marks awarded

How well has your child structured and organised their writing?

The story starts with dialogue to make an effective opening, and has a clearly defined structure. Clear use of pronouns (especially *'she'*) avoids confusion, and time markers (such as *'before', 'at that minute'*) show the relationship between events, which are chronologically organised. Sentences are grouped to distinguish action and dialogue and there is a good use of paragraphs. There are some features of Band 2 (e.g. simple, coherent relationship between ideas), while the good use of paragraphs is a Band 4 feature. On balance it should be awarded Band 3 marks.

5 marks awarded

How effectively has your child told the story?

The opening engages the reader's interest and most of the story is reasonably well paced. However, the ending is rushed and rather weak, but it does relate to the plot. The plot itself does not have any twists, although there is an attempt to keep the reader's interest through suspense. Events and dialogue are suitably interwoven. On balance, the story is considered to have many of the features of Band 3.

7 marks awarded

Helping Juliet to develop her writing

All the marks that Juliet scores are those given to Band 3 writing. However, Juliet only scored maximum marks in one section *(How well has your child structured and organised their writing?)*. In the other two sections it was evident that there were areas where Juliet needed to develop further to meet all the requirements of Band 3.

Although Juliet uses capital letters, full stops and question marks correctly, other punctuation is used inconsistently. Juliet often punctuates speech incorrectly, and some commas are missed out. These are two areas where Juliet could be given further help. Specific practice in punctuating speech might be helpful for Juliet. She might also find it useful if she imagines reading her story aloud, as this might help her to notice where commas are needed to indicate a pause. Juliet also has some problems with accuracy in spelling, although she is generally able to make a sensible guess (e.g. 'binocculers'). If Juliet gets into the habit of re-reading her writing, it might help her to notice if she has made mistakes with spelling or punctuation.

Juliet told her story effectively and although the overall structure of the story met the Band 3 criteria in the mark scheme, the ending is rather weak. You could discuss ways of drawing the threads of the story together more convincingly (what happened at the end of the story to the stranger, the dog and the backpacker?).

HOW TO ASSESS HANDWRITING

There is not a separate test for handwriting, but you should assess legibility and fluency of your child's handwriting in the longer Writing Test (the story 'Missing!').

You should judge the legibility and clarity of the handwriting **throughout the piece**. Additionally, you should consider whether your child's letters are correctly formed and are of an appropriate size.

You should use the following guide to help you to assess your child's handwriting. You should award up to 3 marks for this section of the test.

		Yes	No
BAND 1F	Is the handwriting legible? Are most of the letters of similar size (such as *h, k, l* and *g, y, p*) the **correct** size? Is the spacing between most letters regular? **Award 1 mark if your child's handwriting has most of these features.**	☐ ☐ ☐	☐ ☐ ☐
BAND 2F	Are the letters the right size most of the time? Is the writing joined most of the time? Is the spacing between letters and words appropriate? **Award 2 marks if your child's handwriting has most of these features.**	☑ ☑ ☑	☐ ☐ ☐
BAND 3F	Is the writing joined and legible throughout the story 'Missing!'? Is the joined writing fluent (i.e. do the letter joins seem to 'flow' evenly)? Is the space between letters and words even? Is there a personal style developing in the handwriting? **Award 3 marks if your child's handwriting has most of these features.**	☐ ☐ ☐ ☐	☐ ☐ ☐ ☐

Once you have decided on your child's mark for their handwriting, you should enter it on the Marking grid on page 48.

Marking Juliet's handwriting

Juliet's writing is mostly joined and easy to read throughout the story. There is evidence that Juliet is developing a personal style of handwriting. The space between the letters and words is even. The letters are the right size most of the time, although there are instances where they are not the correct size. For example, in words such as '*called*', '*bothered*' and '*unhappy*' the letters with ascenders (*b, l, h*) are too small. For this reason Juliet would be awarded 2 marks rather than 3 marks for her handwriting.

With a little guided practice focusing on correct letter sizes, Juliet would soon achieve a higher score since she is developing a confident fluent style.

HOW TO MARK THE SPELLING TEST

After your child has completed the test, total up the number of words your child has spelt correctly. This total for the Spelling Test is converted into marks that contribute to the overall level for Writing. Enter the marks from this test on the Marking grid on page 48. Marks should be given as indicated.

Number of correct words	Marks
1–3	1
4–7	2
8–11	3
12–15	4
16–18	5
19–20	6

IMPROVING YOUR CHILD'S SPELLING AT KEY STAGE 2

During Key Stage 2 your child should develop his/her skills in spelling. The Literacy Strategy sets out words that children should learn each year they are in primary school. You could check that your child knows the Year 5 and 6 spelling list. Spelling is best learnt when both phonic strategies (sound) and visual strategies (recognising groups of letters) are used.

In the early stages of learning to spell, children should learn to memorise short common words, e.g. *get, went*. Then they should learn to match sounds to letters – this should help them to spell simple words.

As your child becomes more aware of the relationship between sounds and letters, you should help him or her to see that patterns exist. These include:

- the effect of doubling the vowel, e.g. 'ee' as in *sheep, sleep, freeze*
- how certain vowels and consonants combine, e.g. 'ar' as in *car, card, hard*
- how some consonants combine to make particular sounds, e.g. 'ch' as in *chain, choice, chase*
- how a silent 'e' affects a vowel, e.g. *hop/hope, bit/bite, car/care*
- how two vowels combine to give a particular sound, e.g. 'oi' as in *oil, boil, toil*
- how the grouping of two or more letters gives a particular sound, e.g. 'igh' as in *sigh, high, slight*
- how words that have long vowel sounds such as *journey* need to be committed to the visual memory
- how words with double consonants need to be memorised, e.g. *commented*.

Answers: Spelling

Your child should also develop a visual sense of how words 'look', and consider letter sequences in more complex words. Your child needs to get used to considering whether a word 'looks right'.

A useful way to help your child to memorise a spelling is to use the routine of 'Look, Cover, Write, Check':

Look   at a word and identify phonic patterns or sequences of letters within the word.

Cover   the word, but try to memorise the spelling.

Write   the spelling down.

Check   whether the written word is spelt correctly, identify any mistakes and then try again.

Determining your child's level

FINDING YOUR CHILD'S LEVEL IN READING AND WRITING

When you have marked your child's Reading Test, enter the marks scored for each section of the test on the Marking grid overleaf. Then add them up.

Using this total for the Reading Test, look at the chart below to determine your child's level for Reading.

Reading

Below Level 3	Level 3	Level 4	Level 5	Gifted & Talented
up to 10	11–22	23–35	36–45	46+

When you have marked your child's Writing (and Handwriting) and Spelling Tests, enter the marks scored for each section on the Marking grid overleaf. Then add them up.

Using the total for all three tests (two for Writing and one for Spelling), look at the chart below to determine your child's overall level for Writing.

Writing (including Handwriting and Spelling)

Below Level 3	Level 3	Level 4	Level 5	Gifted & Talented
up to 18	19–30	31–38	39–47	48+

FINDING YOUR CHILD'S OVERALL LEVEL IN ENGLISH

After you have worked out separate levels for Reading and Writing, add up your child's total marks. Use the total and the chart below to determine your child's overall level in English. The chart also shows you how your child's level in these tests compares with the target level for his/her age group.

Total for Reading and Writing

Below Level 3	Level 3	Level 4	Level 5	Gifted & Talented
up to 29	30–53	54–74	75–93	94+
Working towards target level for age group		Working at target level	Working beyond target level	

Marking grid

Reading Pages 28–33

Section	Marks available	Marks scored
Camping and Survival	23	13
Island of the Blue Dolphins	24	13
Camping and Survival and *Island of the Blue Dolphins*	3	3
TOTAL	**50**	37

Writing Pages 34–45

Section	Marks available	Marks scored
How well has your child used sentences and punctuation in the 'Missing!' story?	8	
How well has your child structured and organised their writing of the 'Missing!' story?	8	
How effectively has your child told the 'Missing!' story?	12	
How well has your child organised their writing and used grammar and punctuation in the 'Lost!' notice?	5	
How well has your child written the 'Lost!' notice?	8	
Handwriting mark (from the 'Missing!' story)	3	
Spelling Test	6	
TOTAL	**50**	

English Booklet

Level 3–5

CONTENTS

Camping and Survival

Choosing a site

Great care should be taken when choosing a site. You will presumably stay there for at least one night and want to make sure that you are as comfortable as possible.

The tent should be pitched on level ground, which will take your pegs to a stable depth, without humps or bumps under the groundsheet. The site should be well drained and far enough away from bogs or rivers in case of flooding. There is no fun in having to get up in the dark hours to deal with a flood or a collapsed tent. Choose a site close to a suitable water supply which is important for drinking, cooking and washing. The tent should be protected from the prevailing wind.

Safety first

- Don't pitch your tent under trees. A branch may break off and fall on you.

- Beware of falling rocks when pitching next to a rocky hillside.

- Make sure your site isn't likely to be invaded by cattle.

- Camp far enough above a river or stream in case of flooding.

- If camping on a beach, make sure you are above the high tide mark.

Living in a tent

Living in a tent for any length of time can mean living in difficult conditions. It takes care and planning to manage comfortably, particularly if the weather turns bad. It is very easy to become sloppy. It usually develops due to your own laziness and stupidity, can worsen rapidly and is depressing and even potentially dangerous for the tent's occupants.

Organization and tidiness are essential and are particularly important in wet weather. Always be prepared for the worst, and have a regular routine worked out for pitching, striking camp and dealing with difficult situations quickly as they arise.

Keeping order

- On arrival get the tent pitched as soon as possible. Then sort out your cooking arrangements.

- Lay out your sleeping bag and mat so that you sleep with your head uphill. Keep a torch ready to hand.

- Don't take any more out of your backpack than is necessary. Anything not in use should be kept in the pack. This can be stored between the flysheet and the inner tent.

- Any gear stored inside the tent must always be kept neatly in the same place.

- Take hiking boots off before you go into the tent. Apart from bringing in mud and wet, they can damage the groundsheet.

- Always remove wet clothing before going into a tent.

- Keep the tent clean inside, and be ready to wipe up spills. Gather all litter immediately, and store under the flysheet.

- Don't crowd into a tent or move around clumsily. If the inner tent is pushed against the flysheet, it may let in rain.

What to eat

You will need to eat more than usual while you're living in the open and carrying a backpack. The hillier it is the more energy you will use, and the more you should eat. On a short camping expedition a normal diet should be all right, with plenty of energy-giving carbohydrate foods, lots of liquid and a reasonable amount of salt to prevent dehydration. On longer expeditions a properly balanced diet must be worked out using specialist advice. You will have to carry all or some of your food, so light weight and compactness are important. Tins and bottles are unsuitable. Too much food is unnecessary weight, but you must not go hungry. Daily menus should be worked out in advance, each day's rations stored in its own plastic bags. Food for general use can be stored separately.

Dried foods

Dried foods are compact and very light to carry. They are either prepared by boiling in water, or simpler still by adding hot water. One-pot meals of this kind are uncomplicated, easy to serve hot and don't involve much washing up. Make sure you choose food that you like. Dried stews provide good liquid nourishment and can be served with fresh vegetables and sauces, so don't be afraid to experiment. Note that a packet that 'Serves 2' probably only serves one on a camping trip when appetites are much healthier.

Backwoods cooking

Backwoods cooking should only be practised under proper adult supervision, on a site where it is allowed. To make a Fiji oven you dig a hole in the ground, build a fire at the bottom, light it and rake it out when almost burnt through. You then stack the layers and wait six hours for the food to cook through.

— earth
— cabbage leaves
— food
— cabbage leaves
— hot stones
— hot embers

Fiji oven

Tricks of the backwoods

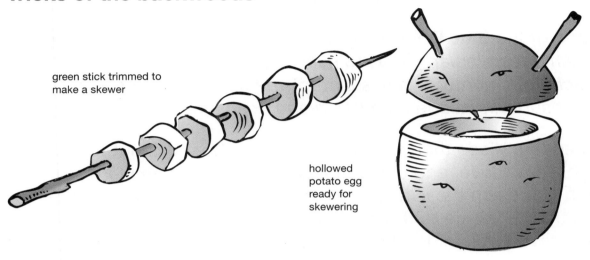

green stick trimmed to make a skewer

hollowed potato egg ready for skewering

Skewers made from green wood can be used to cook over the hot embers of an open fire. Never use yew, laurel, holly, elm or other trees known to be poisonous. Check this locally before you set out. Try a kebab of meat or vegetables, baked fruit such as apples, a hollowed out potato with an egg inside or a breadstick made from self-raising flour and water wrapped round the skewer. A green forked stick with ends twisted into a circle and covered with silver foil can be used as a frying pan. When you've finished, a washing bowl can be made by lining a hole with plastic and weighing down the edges with stones.

foil frying pan

washing bowl

7

Island of the Blue Dolphins

Island of the Blue Dolphins *is the true story of Karana, a 12-year-old American Indian girl, who escapes death at the hands of treacherous hunters. In this extract she explains how she set about surviving alone on a harsh and desolate island.*

I needed a place that was sheltered from the wind, not too far from Coral Cove, and close to a good spring. There were two such places on the island – one on the headland and the other less than a league to the west. The headland seemed to be the more favourable of the two, but since I had not been to the other for a long time I decided to go there and make certain.

The spring was better than the one near the headland, being less brackish and having a steadier flow of water. Besides, it was much easier to reach, since it came from the side of a hill and not from a ravine as the other one did. It was also close to the cliff and a ridge of rocks which would shelter my house.

The rocks were not so high as those on the headland and therefore would give me less protection from the wind, yet they were high enough, and from them I could see the north coast and Coral Cove.

The thing that made me decide on the place to build my house was the sea elephants.

The bull is very large and often weighs as much as thirty men. The cows are much smaller, but they make more noise than the bulls, screaming and barking through the whole day and sometimes at night. The babies are noisy, too.

On this morning the tide was low and most of the animals were far out, just hundreds of specks against the waves, yet the noise they made was deafening.

The morning was fresh from the rain. The smell of the tide pools was strong. Sweet odours came from the wild grasses in the ravines and from the sand plants on the dunes. I sang as I went down the trail to the beach and along the beach to the sandspit. I felt that the day was an omen of good fortune.

It was a good day to begin my new home.

Many years before, two whales had washed up on the sandspit. Most of the bones had been taken away to make ornaments, but ribs were still there, half-buried in the sand.

These I used in making the fence. One by one I dug them up and carried them to the headland. They were long and curved, and when I had scooped out holes and set them in the earth they stood taller than I did.

I put the ribs together with their edges almost touching, and standing so that they curved outward, which made them impossible to climb. Between them I wove many strands of bull kelp, which shrinks as it dries and pulls very tight. I would have used seal sinew to bind the ribs together, for this is stronger than kelp, but wild animals like it and soon would have gnawed the fence down.

For a place to go in and out, I dug a hole under the fence just wide enough and deep enough to crawl through. The bottom and sides I lined with stones. On the outside I covered the hole with a mat woven of brush to shed the rain, and on the inside with a flat rock which I was strong enough to move.

I was able to take eight steps between the sides of the fence, which gave me all the room I would need to store the things I gathered and wished to protect.

I built the fence first because it was too cold to sleep on the rock and I did not like to sleep in the shelter I had made until I was safe from the wild dogs.

The house took longer to build than the fence because it rained many days and because the wood which I needed was scarce. There were only a few trees in the ravines and these were small and crooked. It was very hard to find one that would make a good pole. I searched many days, going out early in the morning and coming back at night, before I found enough for the house.

I used the rock for the back of the house and the front I left open since the wind did not blow from this direction. The poles I made of equal length, using fire to cut them as well as a stone knife which caused me much difficulty because I had never made such a tool before. There were four poles on each side, set in the earth, and twice that many for the roof. These I bound together with sinew and covered with female kelp, which has broad leaves.

While I was building the fence and the house, I ate shellfish and perch which I cooked on a flat rock. Afterwards I made two utensils. Along the shore there were stones that the sea had worn smooth. Most of them were round, but I found two with hollow places in the centre which I deepened and broadened by rubbing them with sand. Using these to cook in, I saved the juices of the fish which are good and were wasted before.

For cooking seeds and roots I wove a tight basket of fine reeds, which was easy because I had learned how to do it from my sister Ulape. After the basket had dried in the sun, I gathered lumps of pitch on the shore, softened them over the fire, and ribbed them on the inside of the basket so that it would hold water. By heating small stones and dropping them into a mixture of water and seeds in the basket I could make gruel.

I made a place for fire in the floor of my house, hollowing it out and lining it with rocks. In the village of Ghalas-at we made new fires every night, but now I made one fire which I covered with ashes when I went to bed. The next night I would remove the ashes and blow on the embers. In this way I saved myself much work.

There were many grey mice on the island and now that I had food to keep from one meal to the other, I needed a safe place to put it. On the face of the rock, which was the back wall of my house, were several cracks as high as my shoulder. These I cut out and smoothed to make shelves where I could store my food and the mice could not reach it.

By the time winter was over and grass began to show green on the hills, my house was comfortable. I was sheltered from the wind and rain and prowling animals. I could cook anything I wished to eat. Everything I wanted was there at hand.

Spelling Test Level 3–5

PARENT'S GUIDE TO THE SPELLING TEST

Your child's version of the Spelling Test is printed on page 27. Your child has to write down the missing words in his or her version as you read the story aloud. The full text of the story is printed overleaf and you may detach this page. The words printed in **bold italics** are the words your child will have to spell.

Go through the instructions on page 26 together, then read the text on the following page aloud. Read the story the first time without stopping. Then read it a second time, pausing in the appropriate places to allow your child to write down the missing words in his or her version.

STORY TO READ ALOUD

You have probably often **heard** people say that food always tastes better out of doors.

Whether it's because of the open air or because you're **especially** hungry after walking, it certainly seems to be true that campers usually have a **healthy** appetite.

If you are camping for any **length** of time, you will need to cook, or at least heat, food and water while you are away from home. Here is some basic advice about **preparing** a meal.

Be sure that you take **particular** care when starting a fire, **selecting** your spot so that there is no risk to surrounding **countryside**. Never **leave** your fire unattended in any circumstances. A moment of **carelessness** can give rise to a major fire, which may **destroy** trees, plants, wildlife and even homes.

You may **choose** to cook simply, heating up **packet** meals or frying eggs and bacon, or you may wish to do some real 'backwoods cooking'. **Although** it sounds rather strange, food will cook slowly if it is first heated **thoroughly**, then buried in the ground with hot coals or embers. Of course, the food should be in a container or **wrapped** in foil. You don't want to eat a **mouthful** of earth!

Finally, don't **forget** the washing up. There's no need to carry a bowl, as you can **scoop** out a hole in the ground and line it with a plastic bag.

Practice Papers

Key Stage 2
National Tests

ENGLISH

First published 1995
Reprinted 1996 (twice), 1997, 1998
Revised 1995, 1997 (twice), 1998, 1999, 2001, 2002, 2003

Text: © Jenny Bates 2002
Design and illustrations: © Letts Educational Ltd 2002

Series editor: Bob McDuell

British Library Cataloguing in Publication Data
A CIP record for this book is available from the British Library

ISBN 1 84315 059 X

Cover design by 2idesign, Cambridge
Cover logo by Starfish Design for Print, London
Project management and typesetting by
Hardlines Ltd, Charlbury, Oxford

Printed in Italy

Acknowledgements
Camping and Survival by Jeremy Evans, Heinemann (Random House); *Island of the Blue Dolphins* by Scott O'Dell, published by Puffin, reprinted with permission.

Letts Educational Ltd
The Chiswick Centre
414 Chiswick High Road
London
W4 5TF
Telephone: 020 8996 3333
Fax: 020 8742 8390
email: mail@lettsed.co.uk
website: www.letts-education.com

Letts Educational Limited is a division of Granada Learning Limited, part of Granada plc.